MINDFULNESS WHILE

PLAYING MUSIC

PRISCILLA AN

T0014383

childsworld.com

The Child's World
childsworld.com

Published by The Child's World®
800-599-READ · www.childsworld.com

Photography Credits
Photographs ©: Aleksandar Nakic/iStockphoto, cover, 1,
14–15, 16, 19, 20; Africa Studio/Shutterstock Images, 3;
Wave Break Media/Shutterstock Images 4–5; iStockphoto,
6–7, 8, 11, 12–13; TMC Photos/Shutterstock Images, 22

ISBN Information
9781503869639 (Reinforced Library Binding)
9781503880917 (Portable Document Format)
9781503882225 (Online Multi-user eBook)
9781503883536 (Electronic Publication)
9781645498667 (Paperback)

LCCN 2022951170

Printed in the United States of America

Priscilla An is a children's book
editor and author. She lives in
Minnesota with her rabbit and
likes to practice mindfulness
through yoga.

TABLE OF CONTENTS

CHAPTER 1

MINDFULNESS AND MUSIC 4

CHAPTER 2

CELLO PRACTICE 6

CHAPTER 3

SUPERSTAR 14

Wonder More . . . 21

Mindful Noise . . . 22

Glossary . . . 23

Find Out More . . . 24

Index . . . 24

MINDFULNESS AND MUSIC

Mindfulness is when people are fully connected to their thoughts, feelings, and surroundings. When people practice mindfulness, they are able to feel calm. They can pay attention to the present moment. They are able to slow down. Mindfulness can be helpful when playing or listening to music. When people are mindful, they are able to enjoy music more. They can **focus** on their bodies' movements. It becomes easier to listen to the sounds and the beats of a song.

Mindfulness is a useful tool when playing music.

CELLO PRACTICE

Chloe has a cello concert tomorrow. She will be playing two songs. It will be her first time going up on stage in front of a lot of people. She has been going to her cello class every day to practice. But today, Chloe is making a lot of mistakes. Her fingers are sweaty, and her legs keep shaking as she plays.

Learning to play an instrument requires a lot of practice.

Cellists need to know how to hold the bow correctly.

Mrs. Zhang is Chloe's cello teacher. She tries to help Chloe. But Chloe's fingers keep slipping.

Chloe drops her **bow**.

"Are you feeling OK?" Mrs. Zhang asks. She looks worried.

"I'm a little nervous about tomorrow," Chloe says. "What if I make mistakes like today?" She wipes her sweaty hands on her pants.

"Everyone gets nervous about their first performance," Mrs. Zhang says. "When I played in front of people the first time, I almost got sick on stage!"

Chloe laughs. She cannot imagine her talented teacher being so nervous!

"But the second time I performed, I focused on the music and on my body," Mrs. Zhang says. "We can try practicing that this time. Instead of thinking about tomorrow, think about the music and your movements as you are playing right now."

Chloe closes her eyes and breathes in deeply. She feels the weight of the cello leaning against her body. She straightens her back to let the instrument balance better.

Before, Chloe's whole body was **tense**. She was squeezing her fingers tightly around the bow. Now, she tries to relax her body as she breathes. Chloe tries to hold the bow lightly.

As Chloe slowly breathes out, she starts playing the song. She thinks about how fun the notes are. When she was nervous, she had forgotten that the song was meant to be played at parties and festivals. It was written to be a celebration. She imagines that the notes are dancing. Soon, her body is swinging with the music. As she focuses on the music and her movements, Chloe starts to forget about the concert.

STAGE FRIGHT

Stage fright is when people have a fear of going up on stage. Their hands might shake. They might have a stomachache. Breathing deeply can help. Focusing on the music and on the performance can also help people stay calm.

Practicing mindfulness can help people relax when they play music.

Having fun while playing music can make performing less scary.

When Chloe finishes, Mrs. Zhang gives her a thumbs-up. "You did a great job, Chloe! Try doing the same thing tomorrow. When you practice mindfulness while playing music, you won't be **distracted** by other thoughts. You will be able to focus on your performance."

Chloe now feels ready. Her stomach still flip-flops when she thinks about being the only one on stage. But now Chloe knows she can focus on relaxing her body and breathing deeply. That will help her focus on the music. "Can I try the next song?" Chloe asks Mrs. Zhang, smiling. She feels ready to play anything!

SUPERSTAR

Joel just started learning how to play drums a month ago. He had learned the basic beats and drum patterns in drum class. For homework, his teacher asked the students to try to be **creative**. The students had to choose any song and try to create their own drum pattern.

In a drum kit, each drum and cymbal makes a different sound.

MINDFUL MOVEMENT

When most people think of mindfulness, they think it is about sitting still. Although stillness can be useful, mindfulness can include movement. Whether people are dancing, exercising, or playing music, they can practice mindfulness. While moving, people can focus on their breathing. They can think about how their bodies feel and move.

Learning the basic beats is important for new drummers.

Joel is frustrated. For the past week, his class learned how to read **drum notations** on sheet music. Now, he has to make up his own. He does not know what song to use. He also does not know how to make his own beats. It is hard to be creative!

Joel thinks about when he first started playing drums. He had watched a video of his favorite band playing a song. The drummer looked so cool when she flipped her drumsticks and started drumming. She looked like she was having so much fun! Joel wanted to be like her. He had come to his first drum class wanting to be a superstar.

Joel has an idea. He turns on his favorite song and closes his eyes. He starts to listen.

Instead of thinking about the drumbeats, Joel lets his body react. He moves his body with the music. He taps his feet. He moves his head. Joel waves his drumsticks in the air. He taps them together.

Then he tries using the movements while playing the drums. He adds new beats to the basic ones he knows. He smashes the cymbals. He slams his foot on the bass drum's pedal. He even flips his drumsticks like his favorite drummer. Before he knows it, Joel is having fun.

Listening to music can help people be creative.

Different songs can change the way a person plays an instrument.

Listening to music was a way for Joel to practice mindfulness. He was able to connect to his body and enjoy the music. He stopped feeling frustrated. Joel even played drumbeats he never tried before. He felt like a superstar.

WONDER MORE

Wondering about New Information

How much did you know about mindfulness before reading this book? What new information did you learn? Write down two new facts that this book taught you. Was the new information surprising? Why or why not?

Wondering How It Matters

What is one way being mindful while playing music relates to your life? How do you think being mindful while playing music relates to other kids' lives?

Wondering Why

Focusing on your body's movements is a good mindfulness exercise. Why do you think it is important to notice your body's movements? How might knowing this affect your life?

Ways to Keep Wondering

Learning about mindfulness while playing music can be a complex topic. After reading this book, what questions do you have about it? What can you do to learn more about mindfulness?

MINDFUL NOISE

Choose an instrument. You do not have to know how to play it. If no instruments are available, try to find any object that makes noise. Make sure to get permission before using someone's instrument!

1. Make any kind of sound on the instrument or object.

2. Focus on the sound. Is the sound harsh? Is it smooth? How do you feel when you play that sound?

3. Close your eyes and try again. Did closing your eyes make a difference?

GLOSSARY

bow (BOH) A bow is used to play a stringed instrument, such as the violin or the cello. Chloe focused on how the bow felt in her hands when she was feeling nervous.

creative (kree-AY-tiv) Being creative is making something new and original. Joel's drum teacher asked the students to be creative and make their own drum patterns.

distracted (dih-STRAKT-ed) When people are distracted, they are not able to pay attention to a task. Chloe's mind was distracted by her nervousness.

drum notations (DRUHM noh-TAY-shuhns) Drum notations are notes on a music sheet that tells drummers how to play a song. Joel learned how to read drum notations in class.

focus (FOH-kuss) To focus is to pay special attention to something. Practicing mindfulness can make it easier to focus on making music.

tense (TENSS) Being tense means feeling stiff and tight. When Chloe practiced mindfulness, she noticed that her body was feeling tense.

FIND OUT MORE

In the Library

An, Priscilla. *Mindfulness with Friends.*
Parker, CO: The Child's World, 2024.

Anthony, William. *Mindfulness.*
Minneapolis, MN: Bearport, 2021.

Kinder, Wynne. *Calm: Mindfulness for
Kids.* New York, NY: DK, 2019.

On the Web

Visit our website for links about mindfulness while
playing music:
childsworld.com/links

*Note to Parents, Caregivers, Teachers, and Librarians: We routinely verify our
Web links to make sure they are safe and active sites. So encourage your readers
to check them out!*

INDEX

breathing, 10–13, 16

cello, 6–13
creativity, 14–17

drums, 14–20

focus, 4, 9–13, 16
frustration, 17, 20
fun, 10, 17–18

mindfulness exercises,
9–13, 16, 18–20
movement, 4, 9–10, 16, 18

nerves, 9–10

practicing music, 6, 9–10

relaxing, 10, 11, 13, 18

stage fright, 9, 11